ANIMAL FAMILIES
OF THE WILD

ANIMAL FAMILIES
OF THE WILD

Animal Stories by Roger Caras, Gerald Durrell,
Dan Mannix, James A. Michener, and Farley Mowat

edited by William F. Russell, Ed.D.
with art by John Butler

CROWN PUBLISHERS, INC.
New York

Published by Crown Publishers, Inc., a Random House company, 225 Park Avenue South, New York, New York 10003
CROWN is a trademark of Crown Publishers, Inc.
Manufactured in the United States of America

Library of Congress Cataloging-in-Publication Data
Animal families of the wild : animal stories / by Roger Caras . . . [et al.] ; edited by William F. Russell, with art by John Butler.
      p.   cm.
   Summary: An anthology of nature writing including pieces on penguins, wolves, eagles, and beavers.
   ISBN 0-517-57358-X (trade)   ISBN 0-517-57359-8 (lib. bdg.)   1. Animals—Juvenile literature. 2. Animals in literature—Juvenile literature. [1. Animals] I. Roger Caras. II. Russell, William F., 1945–   III. Butler, John.   QL791.A579   1990   591—dc20   89-22226

10 9 8 7 6 5 4 3 2 1

First Edition

Grateful acknowledgment is given for the following excerpts:
   From *The Whispering Land* by Gerald Durrell. Copyright © 1961 by Gerald Durrell. All rights reserved. Reprinted by permission of Viking Penguin Inc. and Collins Publishers.
   From *Never Cry Wolf* by Farley Mowat. Used by permission of the Canadian publishers, McClelland and Stewart, Toronto.
   From *The Last Eagle* by Daniel P. Mannix. Copyright © 1965, 1966 by Daniel P. Mannix. Reprinted by permission of Harold Matson Company, Inc.
   From *Centennial* by James A. Michener. Copyright © 1974 by Mayjay Productions, Inc. Reprinted by permission of Random House, Inc.
   From *The Endless Migrations* by Roger Caras. Copyright © 1985 by Roger Caras. Reprinted by permission of the publisher, E. P. Dutton, a division of NAL Penguin Inc.

For Pauline—
who loves every furry thing as a friend,
and treats each as her "favor-ite"
                                    —WFR

            To Cath—
            for all the trouble she takes
                                    —JB

CONTENTS

PREFACE

All of us—from the time we are small children right through our adult years—feel a strange kinship with animals. We don't often talk about it, but we experience it almost every day. We see a squirrel or a rabbit or a deer, and we wonder about how it lives or whether it will survive the coming winter. We feel sad when an animal suffers or dies, and we struggle with unsettling problems and moral questions about killing animals for sport, skinning animals for their fur, and bringing animals into the world only to slaughter them for food.

Why do animals have such a hold on us? It is, I think, because we share with them that quality of being alive—that exceptional trait that just may be unique throughout the vastness of the universe. This sense of being alive is, after all, what defines the members of the animal kingdom and sets them apart from the rest of the world. Scientists say that, in order to be animals, creatures must have the capacity for respiration, reproduction, and locomotion, and so insects, fish, birds, and humans are animals but flowers and trees are not. We may talk about a "living" plant or a "dying" shrub, about "growing" vegetables or "killing" weeds, but the life and death of plants is somehow different; the kinship is missing. Surely there is a difference between the compassion we feel for a mallard duck that is brought down by a shotgun blast or even for a caterpillar that we accidentally crush beneath our feet, and our feeling for a tree that falls to a woodsman's axe. Nor do we feel any grief or discomfort picking a bouquet of pretty flowers—far from it—and that is because flowers are not alive in the way that you and I, and mallard ducks and caterpillars, are.

The danger in recognizing this kinship and in sharing this most essential quality with other species is that we too readily assume that we share other qualities and traits as well. We rush to explain animal behavior in human terms and to see animals as acting out their own versions of human life and human lifestyles. Cartoon animals speak human language and have all the emotions and frailties that characterize humans at their best and worst. Circus bears are dressed like ballerinas and are trained to amuse an audience with their awkward impersonations of human dancers. Even some of our best-loved "nature" *films and stories portray the activities of individual animals as fitting into the patterns and routines of human life. This is a common misinterpretation of animal behavior, one that we must watch for and guard against because it is such an easy and comfortable, though erroneous and dangerous, assumption to make. Animals are not little furry humans or flying humans or wild humans. They are creatures that are as unlike you or me as can possibly be, save that one remarkable, unique, shared trait: We are all alive.*

Still, there is much we can learn from animals by seeing them as they truly are—living animal lives and behaving according to their own animal needs. And if we find lessons in their behavior that apply to our lives, then we will have turned the common misinterpretation inside out.

Throughout our history we have learned from animals by adopting or imitating their ways. But we often fail, nevertheless, to find in our observations of animals any inspiration for our families and for our societies. We do not seem to understand the magnitude of the investment that animal societies make in their young, nor the fact that all animals have as their highest priority the nurturing of their offspring, nor the fact that the human animal created its peculiar forms of family and community for precisely this same purpose.

In understanding animals and in studying the ways they live in nature, we gain more than mere insight into our behavior; we actually become more human. You see, of all the things that separate and distinguish humans from animals, there is one undeniable and unmistakable attribute that is ours alone: We are the only species that is able to know about and think about all the other species. Humans alone have the capacity to contemplate how truly remarkable the grand scheme of nature is, to admire its intricacies, to marvel at its uncountable wonders, and—this above all—to know that we are a part of it. Since this characteristic distinguishes and defines human beings, the more of it we have—the more apparent it is in us—the more human we become. When we do not distinguish ourselves in this way, when we fail to think about nature, and to marvel at its majesty, we begin to behave as though we were not part of it, as though we were children who so envy their high-society friends that they despise their own home and parents, and we find ourselves acting ignorantly, destroying what we cannot replace. It is far less likely that someone who is fascinated by the ways of the animal kingdom will needlessly slaughter its inhabitants or thoughtlessly destroy the habitats on which their survival depends.

This is, in fact, the reason I became involved with Animal Families of the Wild. I have always believed and taught that children and adults alike can learn everything they need to know from the world around them, if only they will be curious enough to do so. We can broaden our vocabulary, stimulate our imagination, and develop a keen appreciation for the artful use of language by reading aloud or listening to someone read the masterpieces of our literary heritage. We can learn geography and history from our own travels and from those of others, measurement and proportion from baking a cake, physics and geometry from the movements of objects in the night sky. So, too, can we learn about the kind of life we can choose to lead by observing those around us; we can practice facing difficult choices and rehearse for the most challenging times before they ever come upon us. From the workings of nature, we also can learn some lessons that may affect the relationships we have with others—with our parents, our brothers and sisters, even with our friends and enemies.

In this book you will be encouraged to wonder and to learn, to be curious and to ask questions, to look at your own life—past, present, and future—and see it with the insight and understanding of an outsider. You will be learning about animals, to be sure, but the questions you will ask will concern your own life and the lives of those around you. At the same time, you will be reading or hearing the words of some of the finest writers of natural science in the world today, and you will be seeing each animal through the eyes of John Butler, one of the most gifted illustrators of wildlife in our time. Because their words and his drawings are so compelling, you will want to know more, and to ask more than you can answer, and that will mark the beginning of an education that, I hope, will continue through all the days of your life. To see the natural world as a knowable place, a place brimming with magical wonders, but one that readily yields its secrets to anyone curious enough to inquire about them, is a major step toward learning and understanding. It is a step that only humans can take—and only the most human ever do.

Some parents may choose to read these stories aloud to their young children; other parents will see them as tales that their older children can read and enjoy on their own.

As read-alouds, though, the value of the stories is doubled, for parents will find themselves experiencing the same visions and feelings that these well-crafted works conjure up in their children—with the added benefit of being able to share precious time with their children in a pursuit that is rewarding and enjoyable for both of them.

In either use, though, the excerpts collected here will encourage children of all ages to see animals in a new way, and to see animal families as being strangely like their own.

—William F. Russell

ONE

Animal babies differ greatly in how ready they are at birth to fend for themselves and survive in their world. Some turtles, for example, are born on a sandy beach, crawl to the sea, and begin providing for themselves within minutes of hatching. There are even a few species of birds that come out of their shells fully able and ready to fly. But most animals are helpless when they first enter the world; without the aid of their parents or other sustaining adults, they would surely die within a few hours of birth. In this regard, it is interesting to note that there is no species of newborn on the planet that is so absolutely dependent for so long a period of time as is the human baby.

What is remarkable in this is not that animal parents choose to nourish their babies rather than abandon them, but that parents of all species perform such extraordinary feats in order to provide that required nourishment. In the following excerpt, Gerald Durrell watches a colony of penguins in Argentina as the parents of each newly hatched bird share the exhaustive search for enough food to meet the incessant demands of their young. And as we witness the parental sacrifices made by these birds, we might wonder why families of the wild are so dedicated to the survival of the young, and we might try to imagine our own helpless infancy as well.

It takes an astute and curious observer to see examples of grand schemes in seemingly insignificant occurrences, and Gerald Durrell is certainly that. For years he led numerous expeditions to the most remote regions on earth, capturing exotic specimens for zoos throughout the world, until at last he decided that the pain of having to surrender his acquisitions at the end of each expedition was too much to bear. He then decided to create his own zoo, on the Isle of Jersey in the English Channel, so that he could continue observing and collecting wildlife, while ensuring that they could be protected and cared for at the same time.

Gerald Durrell, as you will see in this excerpt from The Whispering Land, is also a gifted writer. He relates each activity with a warmth and humor that invites us to care about what we are seeing through his eyes. He describes this vast colony of penguins, for example, as being "like a sea of pygmy headwaiters," and he draws us into feeling for the plight of one infant distinct from the entire mass, one child whose survival depended upon acquiring for herself the necessities of life that were provided outright to offspring who happened to be born into more advantaged circumstances.

Gerald Durrell has written dozens of books about his adventures acquiring and protecting wildlife, among the most popular being My Family and Other Animals, A Zoo in My Luggage, Two in the Bush, Catch Me a Colobus, and Beasts in My Belfry. A more purely scientific view of penguin life can be found in the works of America's preeminent bird watcher, Roger Tory Peterson, and in such books as Penguins, by John Sparks and Tony Soper.

PENGUIN COLONY

from *The Whispering Land*

GERALD DURRELL

A head of us the low brown scrub petered out, and in its place was a great desert of sun-cracked sand. This was separated from the sea beyond by a crescent-shaped ridge of white sand dunes, very steep and some two hundred feet high. It was in this desert area, protected from the sea wind by the encircling arm of the dunes, that the penguins had created their city. As far as the eye could see on every side the ground was pockmarked with nesting burrows, some a mere half-hearted scrape in the sand, some several feet deep. These craters made the place look like a small section of the moon's surface seen through a powerful telescope. In among these craters waddled the biggest collection of penguins I had ever seen, like a sea of pygmy head-waiters, solemnly shuffling to and fro as if suffering from fallen arches due to a lifetime of carrying overloaded trays. Their numbers were prodigious,* stretching to the further-most horizon, where they twinkled black and white in the heat haze. It was a breathtaking sight. Slowly we drove through the scrub until we reached the edge of this gigantic honeycomb of nest burrows and then we stopped and got out of the Land Rover.

*prodigious [pro-DIJ-us]: huge; enormous

We stood and watched the penguins, and they stood and watched us with immense respect and interest. As long as we stayed near the vehicle they showed no fear. The greater proportion of birds were, of course, adult; but each nesting burrow contained one or two youngsters, still wearing their baby coats of down, who regarded us with big melting dark eyes, looking rather like plump and shy debutantes† clad in outsize silver-fox furs. The adults, sleek and neat in their black-and-white suits, had red wattles around the base of their beaks, and bright predatory street-peddler eyes. As you approached them they would back toward their burrows,

†debutantes [DEB-you-tahnts]: young women who are making their formal entrance into high society

6

twisting their heads from side to side in a warning display, until sometimes they would be looking at you completely upside down. If you approached too close they would walk backward into their burrows and gradually disappear, still twisting their heads vigorously. The babies, on the other hand, would let you get within about four feet of them, and then their nerve would break and they would turn and dive into the burrow, so that their great fluffy behinds and frantically flapping feet was all that could be seen of them. . . .

The first thing that became obvious was that most of the movement in the colony was due to adult birds. A great number stood by the nest-burrows, obviously doing sentry duty with the young, while among them vast numbers of other birds passed to and fro, some making their way toward the sea, others coming from it. The distant sand dunes were freckled with the tiny plodding figures of penguins, either climbing the steep slopes or sliding down them. This constant trek to and fro to the sea occupied a large portion of the penguins' day, and it was such a tremendous feat that it deserves to be described in detail. By carefully watching the colony, day by day, during the three weeks we lived among it, we discovered that this is what happened:

Early in the morning one of the parent birds (either male or female) would set out toward the sea, leaving its mate in charge of the nestlings. In order to get to the sea the bird had to cover about a mile and a half of the most grueling and difficult terrain imaginable. First they had to pick their way through the vast patchwork of nesting burrows that made up the colony, and when they reached the edge of this—the suburbs, as it were—they were faced by the desert area, where the sand was caked and split by the sun into something resembling a gigantic jigsaw puzzle. The sand in this area would, quite early in the day, get so hot that it was painful to touch, and yet the penguins would plod dutifully across it, pausing frequently for a rest, as though in a trance. This used to take them about half an hour. But when they reached the other side of the desert they were faced with another obstacle, the sand dunes. These towered over the diminutive* figures of the birds like a snow-white chain of Himalayan mountains, two hundred feet high, their steep sides composed of fine, loose shifting sand. We found it difficult enough to negotiate these dunes, so it must have been far worse for such an ill-equipped bird as a penguin.

*diminutive [dih-MINN-you-tiv]: very small; tiny

When they reached the base of the dunes they generally paused for about ten minutes to have a rest. Some just sat there, brooding, while others fell forward onto their tummies and lay there panting. Then, when they had rested, they would climb sturdily to their feet and start the ascent. Gathering themselves, they would rush at the slope, obviously hoping to get the worst of the climb over as quickly as possible. But this rapid climb would peter out about a quarter of the way up; their progress would slow down, and they would pause to rest more often. As the gradient grew steeper and steeper they would eventually be forced to flop down on their bellies and tackle the slope that way, using their flippers to assist them in the climb. Then, with one final, furious burst of speed, they would triumphantly reach the top, where they would stand up straight, flap their flippers in delight, and then flop down onto their tummies for a ten-minute rest. They had reached the halfway mark and, lying there on the knife-edge top of the dune, they would see the sea, half a mile away, gleaming coolly and enticingly. But they had still to descend the other side of the dune, cross a quarter of a mile of scrubland and then several hundred yards of shingle beach before they reached the sea.

Going down the dune, of course, presented no problem to them, and they accomplished this in two ways, both equally amusing to watch. Either they would walk down, starting very sedately* and getting quicker and quicker the steeper the slope became, until they were galloping along in the most undignified way, or else they would slide down on their tummies, using their wings

*sedately [seh-DATE-lee]: calmly; in a deliberate manner

and feet to propel their bodies over the surface of the sand exactly as if they were swimming. With either method they reached the bottom of the dune in a small avalanche of fine sand, and they would get to their feet, shake themselves, and set off grimly through the scrub toward the beach. But it was the last few hundred yards of beach that seemed to make them suffer most. There was the sea, blue, glittering, lisping seductively on the shore, and to get to it they had to drag their tired bodies over the stony beach, where the pebbles crunched and wobbled under their feet, throwing them off balance. But at last it was over, and they ran the last few feet to the edge of the waves in a curious crouching position, then suddenly straightened up and plunged into the cool water. For ten minutes or so they twirled and ducked in a shimmer of sun ripples, washing the dust and sand from their heads and wings, fluttering their hot, sore feet in the water in ecstasy, whirling and bobbing, disappearing beneath the water and popping up again like corks. Then, thoroughly refreshed, they would set about the stern task of fishing, undaunted by the fact that they would have to face that difficult journey once again before the food they caught could be delivered to their hungry young.

Once they had plodded their way—full of fish—back over the hot terrain to the colony, they would have to start on the hectic job of feeding their ravenous* young. This feat resembled a cross between a boxing- and an all-in wrestling-match, and was fascinating and amusing to watch. There was one family that

*ravenous [RAV-en-us]: extremely hungry; famished

lived in a burrow close to the spot where we parked the Land Rover each day, and both the parent birds and their young got so used to our presence that they allowed us to sit and film them at a distance of about twenty feet, so we could see every detail of the feeding process very clearly. Once the parent bird reached the edge of the colony, it had to run the gauntlet of several thousand youngsters before it reached its own nest-burrow and babies. All these youngsters were convinced that, by launching themselves at the adult bird in a sort of tackle, they could get it to regurgitate† the

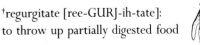

†regurgitate [ree-GURJ-ih-tate]: to throw up partially digested food

food it was carrying. So the adult had to avoid the attacks of these fat, furry youngsters by dodging to and fro like a skillful halfback on a football field. Generally the parent would end up at its nest-burrow, still hotly pursued by two or three strange chicks, who were grimly determined to make it produce food. When it reached home the adult would suddenly lose patience with its pursuers, and, rounding on them, would proceed to beat them up in no uncertain fashion, pecking at them so viciously that large quantities of the babies' fluff would be pecked away and float like thistledown across the colony.

Having routed the strange babies, it would then turn its attention to its own chicks, who were by now attacking it in the same way as the others had done, uttering shrill, wheezing cries of hunger and impatience. It would squat down at the entrance to the burrow and stare at its feet pensively,* making motions like someone trying to stifle an acute attack of hiccups. On seeing this the youngsters would work themselves into a frenzy of delighted anticipation, uttering their wild, wheezing cries, flapping their wings frantically, pressing themselves close to the parent bird's body, and stretching up their beaks and clattering them against the adult's. This would go on for perhaps thirty seconds, when the parent would suddenly—with an expression of relief—regurgitate vigorously, plunging its beak so deeply into the gaping mouths of the youngsters that you felt sure it would never be able to pull its head out again. The babies, satisfied and apparently not stabbed from stem to stern by the delivery of the first course, would squat down on their plump behinds and meditate for a while, and their parent would seize the opportunity to have a quick wash and brushup, carefully preening its breast feathers, picking minute pieces of dirt off its feet, and running its beak along its wings with a clipperlike motion. Then it would yawn, bending forward like someone attempting to touch his toes, wings stretched out straight behind, beak

*pensively [PEN-siv-lee]: in a quiet, thoughtful way; dreamily; wistfully

gaping wide. Then it would sink into the trancelike state that its babies had attained some minutes earlier. All would be quiet for five minutes or so, and then suddenly the parent would start its strange hiccuping motions again and pandemonium* would break out im-

*pandemonium [pan-dih-MOE-nee-um]: wild uproar and utter chaos

mediately. The babies would rouse themselves from their digestive reverie and hurl themselves at the adult, each trying its best to get its beak into position first. Once more each of them in turn would be apparently stabbed to the heart by

the parent's beak, and then once more they would sink back into somnolence.*

*somnolence [SAHM-no-lence]: drowsiness; sleepiness

The parents and young who occupied this nest-burrow where we filmed the feeding process were known, for convenient reference, as the Joneses. Quite close to the Joneses' establishment was another burrow that contained a single, small, and very undernourished-looking chick whom we called Henrietta. Henrietta was the product of an unhappy home life. Her parents were, I suspected, either dim-witted or just plain idle, for they took twice as long as any other penguins to produce food for Henrietta, and then only in such minute quantities that she was always hungry. An indication of her parents' habits was the slovenly nest-burrow, a mere half-hearted scrape, scarcely deep enough to protect Henrietta from any inclement weather, totally unlike the deep, carefully dug villa-residence of the Jones family. So it was not surprising that Henrietta had a big-eyed, half-starved, ill-cared-for look about her that made us feel very sorry for her. She was always on the lookout for food, and as the Jones parents had to pass her front door on their way to their own neat burrow, she always made valiant attempts to get them to regurgitate before they reached home.

These efforts were generally in vain, and all Henrietta got for her pains was a severe pecking that made her fluff come out in great clouds. She would retreat, disgruntled, and

with anguished eye watch the two disgustingly fat Jones babies
wolfing down their food. But one day, by accident, Henrietta
discovered a way to pinch* the Jones family's food without

any unpleasant repercussions. She
would wait until the parent Jones had
started the hiccuping movements as

*pinch: steal

a preliminary to regurgitation and the baby Joneses were
frantically gyrating around, flapping their wings and wheezing,
and then, at the crucial moment, she would join the group,
carefully approaching the parent bird from behind. Then,
wheezing loudly and opening her beak wide, she would thrust
her head either over the adult's shoulder, as it were, or under
its wing, but still carefully maintaining her position behind
the parent so that she should not be recognized. The parent
Jones, being harried† by its gaping-mouthed brood, its mind

fully occupied with the task of re-
gurgitating a pint of shrimps, did not
seem to notice the introduction of a
third head into the general melee‡
that was going on around it. And
when the final moment came it

†harried [HAIR-eed]: annoyed or
tormented as if by constant attacks

‡melee [MAY-lay]: a confused
fight or free-for-all

would plunge its head into the first gaping beak that was
presented, with the slightly desperate air of an airplane pas-
senger seizing his little brown paper bag at the onset of the
fiftieth air pocket. Only when the last spasm had died away,
and the parent Jones could concentrate on external matters,
would it realize that it had been feeding a strange offspring,

and then Henrietta had to be pretty nifty on her great flat feet to escape the wrath. But even if she did not move quickly enough and received a beating for her iniquity,* the smug look on her face seemed to argue that it was worth it.

*iniquity [in-ICK-quit-ee]: wickedness; sinfulness

TWO

When we think of the many kinds of animals that cannot fend for themselves immediately after birth, we begin to see families of the wild operating at their most basic level. Without the protection of their parents, animal infants would become the food that sustains other creatures in nature; without the nourishment provided by their parents, the infants would surely starve. Indeed, these outcomes are common throughout the animal kingdom, es-

pecially for infants whose parents are trapped or killed. But unless the knowledge and skill in how to avoid predators and how to locate food is passed on to the young, they will never live long enough to become parents themselves.

Do animal parents actually teach *their children the lessons they will need to sustain themselves in the wild? Not in the sense that we commonly use the word* teach. *But they do draw out their children's own natural abilities and instincts; they do provide structured opportunities for their children to become everything they can be and to make use of the special talents that set them apart from other animals. A mother eagle does not "teach" her eaglets to fly, but she does model the behavior for them, and she does hold food out over the edge of the nest so that they will leap out after it and be forced to discover that their wings can prevent them from plummeting into the canyon below. An otter or a sea lion does not "teach" her babies to swim, but she does carry them out into the water on her back and then loosen their grasp so that they are on their own with only their natural ability to keep them from drowning.*

In the excerpt that follows, Farley Mowat watches as the parents of four wolf cubs herd some caribou toward the youngsters so that the cubs can get their first taste of the hunt. This "schooling" of the young was only one of the ways of the wolf that Mowat learned during the fascinating adventure he describes in Never Cry Wolf. *On his solitary expedition to the Barren Lands of northern Canada, Mowat so wanted to understand the ways of wolves that he adopted their lifestyle and even their eating habits. He writes in an often humorous, always provoking way about his own experiences learning to take "wolf* naps" and to eat a diet based on mice, just as the creatures he was studying did.

He introduces us to Angeline and George—his names for the parents of the four cubs in the excerpt—and to their companion, whom he calls Uncle Albert. He tells us of his Eskimo friend Ootek, who had spent his life observing wolves and who claimed to be able to speak their language. Never Cry Wolf is a wonderful adventure for anyone who is interested in learning about how animals actually behave in their natural environment, as well as how different this behavior is from what we have been led to believe. At the same time, it chastises humankind more than does Mowat's earlier classic, The Dog Who Wouldn't Be, but less than his later exposé of the way we have destroyed the land and sea animals along the North Atlantic Coast, Sea of Slaughter—both of which should be on the reading list of anyone who is concerned about the preservation of animal life.

WOLF PUP

from *Never Cry Wolf*

FARLEY MOWAT

The pups had left the summer den and, though they could not keep up with Angeline and the two males on prolonged hunts, they could and did go along on shorter expeditions. They had begun to explore their world, and those autumnal months must have been among the happiest of their lives.

When Ootek and I returned to Wolf House Bay after our travels through the central plains, we found that our wolf family was ranging widely through its territory and spending the days wherever the hunt might take it.

Within the limits imposed upon me by my physical abilities and human needs, I tried to share that wandering life, and I, too, enjoyed it immensely. . . .

On one such warm and sunlit day I made my way north from the den esker* along the crest of a range of hills which overlooked a great valley, rich in forage, and much used by the caribou as a highway south.

A soot-flecking of black specks hung in the pallid† sky above the valley—flocks of ravens following the deer herds. Families of ptarmigan‡ cackled at me from clumps of dwarf shrub. Flocks of old squaw ducks, almost ready to be off for distant places, swirled in the tundra ponds.

Below me in the valley rolled a sluggish stream of caribou, herd after herd grazing toward the south, unconscious, yet directly driven by a knowledge that was old before we ever knew what knowledge was.

Some miles from the den esker I found a niche§ at the top of a high cliff overlooking the valley, and here I settled myself in comfort, my back against the rough but sun-warmed rock, my knees drawn up under my chin, and my binoculars leveled at the living stream below me.

*esker [ESS-ker]: a narrow and rocky ridge formed by a glacial stream; these steep ridges bordered the wolves' summer den

†pallid [PAL-id]: pale; not brightly colored

‡ptarmigan [TAR-mih-gan]: a type of grouse that has feathered feet and inhabits cold northern regions

§niche [NITCH or NEESH]: a crevice or cranny

I was hoping to see the wolves and they did not disappoint me. Shortly before noon two of them came into sight on the crest of a transverse ridge some distance to the north. A few moments later two more adults and the four pups appeared. There was some frisking, much nose smelling and tail wagging, and then most of the wolves lay down and took their ease, while the others sat idly watching the caribou streaming by on either side only a few hundred feet away.

I easily recognized Angeline and George. One of the other two adults looked like Uncle Albert; but the fourth, a

rangy dark-gray beast, was a total stranger to me. I never did learn who he was or where he came from, but for the rest of the time I was in the country he remained a member of the band.

Of all the wolves, indeed of all the animals in view including the caribou and myself, only George seemed to feel any desire to be active. While the rest of us sprawled blissfully in the sun, or grazed lethargically* amongst the lichens,† George began to wander restlessly back and forth along the top of the ridge. Once or twice he stopped in front of Angeline but she paid him no attention other than to flop her tail lazily a few times.

Drowsily I watched a doe caribou grazing her way up the ridge on which the wolves were resting. She had evidently found a rich patch of lichens and, though she must have seen the wolves, she continued to graze toward them until not twenty yards separated her from one of the pups. This pup watched her carefully until, to my delight, he got to his feet, stared uneasily over his shoulder to see what the rest of the family was doing, then turned and slunk toward them with his tail actually between his legs.

Not even the restless George, who now came slowly toward the doe, his nose outthrust as he tasted her scent, seemed to disturb her equanimity‡ until the big male wolf, perhaps hurt in his dignity by her unconcern, made a quick feint* in her direction. At that she flung her head high, spun on her ungainly legs, and gallumphed back down the ridge, apparently more indignant than afraid.

*feint [FAINT]: a fake; a movement designed to fool or distract an adversary

Time slipped past, the river of deer continued to flow, and I expected to observe nothing more exciting than this brief interlude between the doe and the wolves, for I guessed that the wolves had already fed, and that this was the usual after-dinner siesta. I was wrong, for George had something on his mind.

A third time he went over to Angeline, who was now stretched out on her side, and this time he would not take "no" for an answer. I have no idea what he said, but it must have been pertinent, for she scrambled to her feet, shook herself, and bounced amiably after him as he went to sniff at the slumbering forms of Uncle Albert and the Stranger. They, too, got the message and rose to their feet. The pups, never slow to join in something new, also roused and galloped over to join their elders. Standing in a rough circle, the whole group of wolves now raised their muzzles and began to howl, exactly as they used to do at the den esker before starting on a hunt.

I was surprised that they should be preparing for a hunt so early in the day, but I was more surprised by the lack of reaction to the wolf chorus on the part of the caribou. Hardly a deer within hearing even bothered to lift its head, and those few who did contented themselves with a brief, incurious

25

look toward the ridge before returning to their placid* graz-ing. I had no time to ponder the matter, for Angeline, Albert, and the Stranger now started off, leaving the pups sitting disconsolately† in a row on the crest, with George standing just ahead of them. When one of the youngsters made an attempt to follow the three adults, George turned on him, and the pup hurriedly rejoined his brothers and sisters.

What little wind there was blew from the south and the three wolves moved off upwind in a tight little group. As they reached the level tundra they broke into a trot, following one another in line, not hurrying, but trotting easily through the groups of caribou. As usual the deer were not alarmed

*placid [PLASS-id]: peaceful; tranquil; calm

†disconsolately [dis-CON-suh-lit-lee]: in a hopelessly sad or gloomy manner

and none took evasive action except when the wolves happened to be on a collision course with them.

The three wolves paid no attention to the caribou either, although they passed many small herds containing numbers of fawns. They made no test runs at any of these groups, but continued purposefully on their way until they were almost abreast the niche where I was sitting. At this point Angeline stopped and sat down while the other two joined her. There was more nose smelling, then Angeline got up and turned toward the ridge where George and the pups still sat.

There were at least two hundred deer between the two groups of wolves, and more were coming constantly into view around the eastern shoulder of the transverse ridge. Angeline's glance seemed to take them all in before she and her companions began to move off. Spreading out to form a line abreast, with intervals of a couple of hundred yards between them so that they almost spanned the whole width of the valley, they now began to run north.

They were not running hard, but there was a new purposefulness to their movements which the deer seemed to recognize; or perhaps it was just that the formation the wolves were using made it difficult for the herds to avoid them in the usual way by running off to one side. In any event herd after herd also began to turn about and move north, until most of the caribou in the valley were being driven back the way they had come.

The deer were clearly reluctant to be driven, and several herds made determined efforts to buck the line; but on each occasion the two nearest wolves converged toward the re-calcitrant* caribou and forced them to continue north. How-

*recalcitrant [ree-KAL-sih-trant]: stubborn; resisting authority or control

ever, three wolves could not sweep the whole width of the valley; the deer soon began to discover that they could swing around the open wings and so resume their southerly progress. Nevertheless, by the time the wolves were nearing the ridge, they were herding at least a hundred deer ahead of them.

Now for the first time the deer showed real signs of nervousness. What had become an almost solid mass of a hundred or more animals broke up into its constituent small bands again, and each went galloping off on its own course. Group after group began to swerve aside, but the wolves no longer attempted to prevent them. As the wolves galloped past each of these small herds, the caribou stopped and turned to watch for a moment before resuming their interrupted journey south.

I was beginning to see what the wolves were up to. They were now concentrating their efforts on one band of a dozen does and seven fawns, and every attempt which this little herd made to turn either left or right was promptly foiled. The deer gave up after a while and settled down to outrun their pursuers in the straightaway.

They would have done it, too, but as they swept past the clump of willows at the end of the ridge a perfect flood of wolves seemed to take them in the flank.

I could not follow events as well as I would have wished because of the distance, but I saw George racing toward a

28

doe accompanied by two fawns. Then, just as he reached them, I saw him swerve away. He was passed by two pups going like gray bullets. These two went for the nearest of the two fawns, which promptly began jinking.* One of the pups, attempting too sharp a turn, missed his footing and tumbled head over heels, but he was up on the instant and away again.

The other pups seemed to have become intermingled with the balance of the deer, and I could not see what they were up to, but as the herd drew away at full gallop the pups appeared in the rear, running hard, but losing ground.

A single fawn now began outdistancing its pursuers too. All four pups were still running flat out, although they no longer had a chance of overtaking any of the deer.

What of the adult wolves meanwhile? When I swung my glasses back to look for them I found George standing exactly where I had seen him last, his tail wagging slowly as he watched the progress of the chase. The other three wolves had by now returned to the crest of the ridge. Albert and the Stranger had lain down to rest after their brief exertions, but Angeline was standing up and watching the rapidly re-treating caribou.

It was half an hour before the pups came back. They were so weary they could hardly climb the ridge to join their elders, all of whom were now lying down relaxing. The pups joined the group and flopped, panting heavily; but none of the adults paid them any heed.

School was over for the day.

THREE

There comes a time in the development of all families of the wild when the children are no longer helpless, and when, in order to fulfill their own destiny, they must leave behind the comfort and security of the den or nest and accept the challenge of making their own way in the world. Sometimes the young animal is eager to strike out alone and chafes for the chance to be free and independent; sometimes the parents have to know when the proper time has come and push the youngster in the direction of maturity. Either event will mark the end of a generation in the life of the species and the faint beginning of another. Now comes the test to see whether the nourishment and lessons that were given so unselfishly by the parents can sustain the children in the do-or-die, win-or-lose, uncompromising world we call nature.

The excerpt that follows is from a book titled The Last Eagle, which focuses on a bald eagle that was born high in an elm tree near Maryland's Chesapeake Bay. After learning how to fly and how to hunt and how to stay out of the range of men with guns, the eaglet, along with his parents, made a long journey to the Florida Everglades, and it is here that our story begins.

Although the tale is fictitious, every activity of the eagles is based on scientific fact and detailed observation. The author, Dan Mannix, spent three months perched atop a sixty-foot steel tower photographing the activities of a nearby family of eagles. You will see, for instance, in his detailed description of the process by which eagles navigate— what we call the "homing instinct"—that this is as close to natural science as fiction can come.

Dan Mannix has written several other books about animals, including All Creatures Great and Small, which recounts his boyhood experiences collecting pets of every type. In two other books he uses the same detailed and scientifically accurate descriptions of fictionalized animal activities that he employs in The Last Eagle. The Fox and the Hound and The Killers (a story about the struggles between a fighting cock and a hawk) are superbly told tales of natural enemies in the wild.

Another good book about the ways of the bald eagle and the

near-extinction of our national bird is George Laycock's Autumn of the Eagle, *while the similar travails of a golden eagle are captured in Kent Durden's* Gifts of an Eagle.

EAGLE FAMILY

from *The Last Eagle*

DAN MANNIX

T he young male was bewildered by the bounty around him. The waterways were teeming with fish, there were vast flocks of slow-flying birds at his mercy, and the shores of the ocean were strewn with crabs, mollusks, and other shellfish. There were also plenty of ospreys* who could be robbed. Even so, he continued to stay near his parents. He was nervous in this new place and, given a choice, would much have preferred to be home again at the familiar nest on the Chesapeake no matter how great the privations.† Still, he was fascinated by this strange new land, even though apprehensive.

At first he dutifully followed his parents on their fishing expeditions. With any luck they would be fully gorged an hour after sunup and spend the rest of the day sitting on a dead mangrove‡ icily regal, splendidly null, barely turning their heads as they surveyed the great savannahs§ laid out around them. In the cool of the late afternoon they would set out again, more to exercise their wings than to do any serious hunting, returning to the mangrove shortly before dark to roost for the night. . . .

His parents rarely hunted ducks, or any other birds, unless the quarry was obviously wounded. Flying with them, however, he noticed that they would often check their course to take after a wigeon,° teal, mallard, or gadwall that seemed perfectly healthy yet after a few seconds' flying proved to be heavy on the wing. Gradually he learned to watch for the slight indications of sluggishness that betrayed these handicapped ones. He also

*ospreys [AH-spreez]: large hawks that feed on fish

†privations [pry-VAY-shuns]: hardships; the lack of comforts or necessities

‡mangrove: a tropical evergreen tree or shrub

§savannahs [suh-VAN-ahz]: grassy, treeless flatlands in the tropics

°wigeon [WIJ-un], teal, mallard, or gadwall: types of ducks

learned when eating them to disregard the gizzard, as it was sure to be full of lead shot. These "puddle ducks" had dabbled in the shallow water of marshes and rivers, scooping up vegetation that contained shot pellets from the annual autumn fusillade.* They were weighed down with lead and had trouble either flying or diving.

*fusillade [FEW-sih-lahd]: a barrage of gunfire; here, referring to the fall duck-hunting season

His great triumph came when he was flying out to sea where the activity of a flock of herring gulls showed him food might be expected. A solitary Canada goose came flapping by, and the eagle took after him in sport. Gradually he overhauled the big bird in a long, stern chase, but as he closed in to bind to his quarry, the goose folded one wing and barrel rolled under his blow. The eagle duplicated the motion, and

for a few moments the two great birds whirled about like blown leaves in an involved game of follow the leader. During one of the turns the eagle found himself below the goose and, turning on his back, seized his quarry from below. As soon as he locked his talons in the big bird, the goose's weight sent him hurtling down toward the water so fast he was unable to slow his descent in spite of his wildly flapping wings. Both eagle and goose hit the water with a splash that sent spray high into the air. The eagle was so proud of his capture that he refused to let go. Instead, he towed the goose nearly half a mile to shore, doused with spray from every swell, and forced to flap constantly with no chance of soaring. When he finally beached his quarry, he was so exhausted he sat beside his bedraggled prey and panted for more than an hour before beginning to feed.

The young eagle spent the next few days recuperating from his supreme effort, living on his gorge, and doing no flying at all. The feat had not been worth the effort involved. From then on he began to sense why his parents would not go to the effort of taking wildfowl unless the quarry were injured.

The immature eagle still had the exuberance of youth and enjoyed hunting for hunting's sake. Yet he began to take note of what quarry could be taken easily and what required an exhausting effort. . . .

When February came, the young eagle noticed that his parents were growing increasingly restless. Often they would spread their wings as though about to take off, only to fold them again and resume their motionless stance. Then they began to make short, aimless flights around the savannahs, occasionally turning on each other with angry cries and rushing together with extended talons. These flare-ups never amounted to anything, yet the immature bird was disturbed. He could not understand what was the matter with his parents. When he attempted to join in their quarrels, both adults turned on him with an entirely unexpected fury, especially his father, who hitherto had always been his ally. Frightened, the young male avoided his parents. He shifted his lookout post from the mangrove and withdrew to a cypress where he remained in injured solitude.

Then one morning there was a strong, mild south wind. Shortly after dawn the young bird saw his parents leave the mangrove and begin to soar in vast, vulture-like circles, going up and up, until he had to cock his head on one side to follow them. Slowly he came to realize that they were moving steadily away toward the north and that this was no casual morning flight. Alarmed, he also took to the air and rung up after them.

The old male picked up a steady breeze blowing north along the Atlantic Coast, and now his flight took on direction and purpose. The female followed, and after her came the immature male. In a long line they headed north.

As the weather grew colder, the speed of the adults increased. They refused to stop for food, and the young bird had to follow for fear of being left behind. Over Cape Hatteras they swept, across Pocomoke Sound, on past Chincoteague

Island. A frenzy seemed to possess them to reach some certain place as soon as possible. Slowly the young eagle developed the same frenzy.

He had been happy in Florida, yet now he realized that always there had been a nagging pain constantly throbbing back of his eyes. Like any steady pain, the eagle had grown used to it and even forgotten it existed. Now as he went north the pain lessened steadily. The relief flooded him with a sense of satisfaction he had never known before.

Inside the eagles' eyes were a series of tissues folded into pleats called the pectens. Each pleat contained a fine network of lymph* tubes. The lymph fluid in these tubes was electrolyte and operated as a conductor of electricity. The earth operates as a giant magnet, the lines of magnetic intensity extending in the forms of arcs from the north magnetic pole. As a nestling, the lymph tubes in the young eagle's pectens had adjusted themselves to the lines of magnetic intensity in the area of Chesapeake Bay. Now that they were returning, the familiar pressure was bringing a surcease† from the nagging feeling of being somehow unbalanced.

*lymph [LIMMF]: a clear, yellowish liquid that removes bacteria from the tissues

†surcease [sir-SEES]: a stop; an end

When the birds reached the vicinity of Rehoboth Beach, a heavy fog moved in. Ordinarily they would have roosted until they had clear weather, but with the growing blessed relief of the pectens, they kept on. Cities, radio towers, and above all high-tension lines were now their deadliest threat, for they could see only a few yards in front of them. Mile by mile the pressure of their pectens registered that they were getting nearer to home. They were on the old, comforting, familiar arc that ran through the site of their home eyrie.*

To find the exact nesting area, they needed another coordinate. The pecten enabled them to discriminate

*eyrie [AIR-ee]: the nest of an eagle or other large bird of prey

between the different elements of a geomagnetic field; to measure "dip angle" and the intensities of the vertical, horizontal, and total field. As the pattern of sensory response would be different for each eye, they could use two of these elements to fix longitude and latitude. The adult male inclined his flight slightly northwest and the others followed, flying almost wingbeat for wingbeat with him.

Now they were within twenty miles or so of the nesting area. The pectens could do no more. The lymph tubes could not pinpoint the nesting tree. Slowly the male dropped, the others tailing him as geese or ducks tail an experienced leader who has the homing instinct so highly developed that he can detect the slightest alterations of the electrolyte fluid. Once they had to zoom up suddenly when a mass of thick pines came rushing at them through the fog, but finally the father was able to bring them down safely into a stand of maples whose bare, broad limbs made an easy landing. Here they spent the night.

When the sun rose, the fog shredded away and there before them lay their old range. Now they could fly by dead reckoning, for with their marvelous memories they knew every landmark for miles around the nest. At once, they started off, and within an hour were back in the eyrie, standing happily in the wet grass sodden from the winter snow and rain.

They were home. If necessary, the young eagle could return equally unerringly to the mangrove tree in the Everglades by flying until his pectens registered the same impulses he had grown to know during the winter sojourn.* But now nothing could have induced him to leave the nesting site. He pranced around the nest, waving his wings and giving eager little cries. . . . His head was clear, the sun was shining, all was right with the world.

*sojourn [SO-jurn]: a temporary stay or visit

It did not long remain so. At best, his parents ignored him. At worst—and matters grew steadily worse—they resented him. Before, his parents had always sat apart from each other, scarcely seeming to know the other was there. Now they sat side by side, the elbows of their wings touching. From time to time they would peck at each other's beaks very softly or even comb the other's head. They seemed to be constantly in the air making great patterns in the sky, coming together, sheering off, fluttering downward together only to break off and rise again.

When he tried to join the games, they turned on him. His father went at him with such ferocity he was hard put to save himself. These attacks were deadly serious. Soon he realized that eventually his father would not be content by merely driving him off; the adult male would kill him.

He could not imagine what had happened. His parents were driven by some impulse far beyond his conception. He was forced from the nest tree; then from the range itself. He wandered alone and rejected, an Ishmael* driven out by his own kin.

He found other pairs of eagles, but these, too, drove him away. He might have returned to Florida, but even there there was no welcome for him and he preferred the bracing cold to the humid warmth.

*Ishmael [ISH-may-ell]: an outcast; a biblical reference to a son of Abraham who was exiled into the wilderness with his mother

The prevailing winds were from the south and he rode them day after day. He glided high over Montauk Point, following the pathway of the sky as a sailing ship would follow the trade winds. He crossed Cape Cod, and now before him were endless seas without sight of land. Still, the breeze held and he had never flown over any stretch of water so great he could not make land. The

†nor'-nor'-east: the compass direction "north-northeast" in sailors' dialect

wind was now nor'-nor'-east† and he rode it unthinkingly.

FOUR

*T*he joys and comforts that are felt by the members of human families must, one would think, be experienced by families of the wild as well. But there is a "family clock" that governs the lives of animal children as they develop. The onset of maturity cannot be extended or delayed, nor can the pleasures of family life be continued beyond the time prescribed by the unalterable demands of nature. In this harsh and unforgiving world, individual differences and preferences count for nothing; the children who can go out on their own must go out on their own; they will find mates and create new generations like themselves, and the species will survive.

Yet within these immutable commands of nature is there not room for individual personalities to carry out the continuation of the species in their own way and to leave their personal stamp on their own time and place? This is the question on which James A. Michener brings his Pulitzer Prize—winning talents to bear in the excerpt that follows. From his exhaustive research about the ways of the beaver he has learned when and where and how beavers and their families do what they do, but here he allows his imagination to suggest why. Here he focuses upon one nameless adolescent female who endures hardships that may remind us of similar misfortunes that all too commonly befall human adolescents. But instead of seeing her as acting out a human drama, we can better use her actions and responses as a stimulus for imagining how we would, or should, respond in similar circumstances, and how much we, too, are driven by forces we do not understand.

We also see in this excerpt, just as in the previous stories about wolves and eagles, an inseparable connection between the concepts of "family" and "home." For many animals, and for many humans as well, each of these concepts helps define the other. A family needs a private space and place in which to develop as a family, and a house or an apartment never seems to fulfill the idea of a "home" until a family dwells therein. This beaver's lodge becomes a home in every sense, and therefore it, just like her family, is worth all the sacrifices she makes to defend it and even to rebuild it again and again.

This story is taken from James A. Michener's novel Centennial, which also includes brief fictional sketches about other species that

inhabited the North American West before the coming of humankind—
the dinosaur, the horse, the buffalo, and the rattlesnake. Other books
that have looked at the lives and habits of beavers in the wild—
including the need to protect and preserve these remarkable creatures—
are the classic Pilgrims of the Wild, by Grey Owl (a name this
British naturalist took when adopted by the Ojibway Indians of
Canada); Hour of the Beaver, by Hope Sawyer Buyukmichi; and
Beaversprite, by Dorothy Richards.

BEAVER LODGE

from *Centennial*

JAMES A. MICHENER

One spring the mother and father beavers in a lodge on a small creek west of the twin pillars made it clear to their two-year-old daughter that she could no longer stay with them. She must fend for herself, find herself a mate, and with him build her own lodge. She was not happy to leave the security in which she had spent her first two years; henceforth she would be without the protection of her hard-working parents and the noisy companionship of the five kits, a year younger than herself, with whom she had played along the banks of the stream and in its deep waters.

Her greatest problem would be to find a young male beaver, for there simply were none in that part of the creek. And so she must leave, or in the end her parents would have to kill her because she was mature enough to work for herself and her space inside the lodge was needed for future batches of babies.

So with apprehension but with instinctive hope, this young female left her family for the last time, turned away from the playful kits, and swam down the tunnel leading to the exit. Gingerly, as she had been taught, she surfaced, poked her small brown nose toward shore, and sniffed for signs of enemies. Finding none, she gave a strong flip of her webbed hind feet, curling her little paws beneath her chin, and started downstream. There was no use going upstream, for there the building of a dam was easier and all the good locations would be taken.

One flap of her hind feet was sufficient to send her cruising along the surface for a considerable distance, and as she went she kept moving her head from side to side, looking for three things: saplings in case she needed food, likely spots to build a dam and its accompanying lodge, and any male beavers that might be in the vicinity.

Her first quest was disappointing, for although she spotted quite a few cottonwoods, which a beaver could eat if need be, she found no aspen or birch or alders, which were her preferred foods. She already knew how to girdle a small tree, strip its bark, and fell it so that she could feed on the upper limbs. She also knew how to build a dam and lay the groundwork for a lodge. In fact, she was a skilled housekeeper, and she would be a good mother, too, when the chance presented itself.

She had gone downstream about a mile when there on the shore, preening* himself, she saw a handsome young male. She studied him for a moment without his seeing her, and she judged correctly that he had chosen this spot for his dam. She surveyed the site and

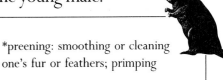

*preening: smoothing or cleaning one's fur or feathers; primping

knew intuitively that he would have been wiser to build it a little farther upstream, where there were strong banks to which it could be attached. She swam toward him, but she had taken only a few powerful strokes of her hind feet when, from a spot she had not noticed, a young female beaver splashed into the water, slapped her tail twice, and came directly at the intruder, intending to do battle. It had taken her a long time to find a mate and she had no intention of allowing anything to disrupt what promised to be a happy family life.

The male on shore watched disinterestedly as his female approached the stranger, bared her powerful front teeth, and prepared to attack. The stranger backed away and returned to the middle of the stream, and the victorious female slapped the water twice with her tail, then swam in triumph back to her unconcerned mate, who continued preening himself and applying oil to his silky coat.

The wandering beaver saw only one other male that day, a very old fellow who showed no interest in her. She ignored him as he passed, and she kept drifting with no set purpose.

As late afternoon came on and she faced her first night away from home, she became nervous and hungry. She climbed ashore and started gnawing desultorily* at a cotton-wood, but her attention was not focused on the food, and this was good, because as she perched there, her scaly tail stretched out behind her, she heard a movement behind a larger tree and looked up in time to spot a bear moving swiftly toward her.

*desultorily [DESS-ull-tore-uh-lee]: in a casual, indifferent way; without a sense of plan or purpose

Running in a broken line, as she had been taught, she evaded the first swipe of the slashing paw, but she knew that if she continued running toward the creek, the bear would intercept her. She therefore surprised him by running parallel to the creek for a short distance, and before he could adjust his lunge to this new direction, she had dived to safety.

She went deep into the water, and since she could stay submerged for eight or nine minutes, this gave her time to swim far from where the bear waited, because even from the bank a bear could launch a powerful swipe which might lift a beaver right onto the bank. When she surfaced, he was far behind her.

Night fell, the time when her family had customarily

played together and gone on short excursions, and she was lonely. She missed the kits and their noisy frolic, and as night deepened she missed the joy of diving deep into the water and finding the tunnel that would carry her to the warm security of the lodge.

Where would she sleep? She surveyed both banks and selected a spot which offered some protection, and there she curled up as close to the water as she could. It was a miserable substitute for a proper lodge, and she knew it.

Three more nights she spent in this wretched condition. The season was passing and she was doing nothing about the building of a dam. This bothered her, as if some great purpose for which she had been bred was going unattended.

But the next day two wonderful things happened, the

second having far more lasting consequences than the first. Early in the morning she ventured into a part of the creek she had not seen before, and as she moved she became aware of a strong and reassuring scent. If it were serious, and not an accident, it would be repeated at the proper intervals, so she swam slowly and in some agitation to the four compass directions, and as she had anticipated, the keen smell was repeated as it should have been. A male beaver, and young at that, had marked out a territory and she was apparently the first female to invade it.

Moving to the middle of the stream, she slapped her tail, and to her joy a fine-looking young beaver appeared on the bank of the creek and looked down into the water. The slapping could have meant that another male had arrived to contest his territory and he was prepared to fight, but when he saw that his visitor was the kind he had hoped to attract, he gave a little bark of pleasure and dived into the stream to welcome her.

With strong sweeps of his webbed feet he darted through the water and came up to her, nudging her nose with his. He was highly pleased with what he found and swam twice around her as if appraising her. Then he dived, inviting her to follow him, and she dived after him, deep into the bottom of the creek. He was showing her where he intended building his lodge, once he found a female to help.

They returned to the surface and he went ashore to fetch some edible bark, which he placed before her. When beavers mated, it was for life, and he was following an established pattern of courtship. The female was eager to indicate her interest, when she noticed that his gaze had left hers and that any fruitful communication had ended.

He was looking upstream, where one of the most beautiful young beavers he had ever seen was about to enter his territory. This female had a shimmering coat and glowing eyes, and she swam gracefully, one kick sending her to the corners of his area, where she checked the markers he had left. Contented that she was in the presence of a serious suitor, she moved languidly* to the center of the area and signaled with her tail.

The young male left his first visitor and with lightning strokes sped to this newcomer, who indicated that

*languidly [LANG-guid-lee]: weakly; slowly; in a listless manner

she was interested in the segment of the creek he had laid out for himself and was willing to move in permanently. In this brief space of time their destiny was determined.

What now to do with the first visitor? When the new female saw her she apprehended immediately what had happened, so she and the male came to where the young beaver waited and started to shove her out of the delimited area. But she had got there first and intended to stay, so she dived at the intruding female and started to assault her, but the male knew what he wanted. He had no desire to settle for second best, so he joined the newcomer, and together they forced the unwanted intruder downstream, and as she disappeared, chattering in rage, they slapped their tails at her and made joyous noises and prepared to build their dam.

The outcast drifted aimlessly and wondered whether she would ever find a mate. How could she build a home? How could she have kits of her own? Bitterly she sought the next miserable place to spend a night.

But as she explored the bank she became aware of a soft sound behind her and was certain it must be an otter, the most fearful of her enemies. She dived deep and headed for any cranny within the bank that might afford protection, and as she flattened herself against the mud she saw flashing through the waters not far distant the sleek, compacted form of an otter on the prowl.

She hoped that his first sweep would carry him downstream, but his sharp eye had detected something. It could have been a beaver hiding against the bank, so he turned in a graceful dipping circle and started back. She was trapped, and in her anxiety, fought for any avenue of escape. As she probed along the bottom of the bank she came upon an opening which led upward. It could well be some dead end from which there was no escape. But whatever it was, it could be no worse than what she now faced, for the otter was returning and she could not swim fast enough to escape him.

She ducked into the tunnel and with one powerful kick sent herself upward. She moved so swiftly that she catapulted through the surface and saw for the first time the secret cave that had formed in the limestone, with a chimney which admitted air and a security that few animals ever found. Soon her eyes became accustomed to the dim light that filtered in from above and she perceived what a marvelous spot this was, safe from otters and bears and prowling wolves. If she built her dam slightly below the cave and constructed her lodge in the body of the creek, attaching it by tunnel to this secret place, and if she then widened the chimney upward and masked its exit so that no stranger could detect it, she would have a perfect home. To complete her delight she found inside the cave and above the water level a comfortable ledge on which she could sleep that night.

Before dawn she was at work. Moving to all the prominent places on shore and to the ledges in the creek, she stopped at each and grabbed a handful of mud. With her other hand she reached to the opening of her body where two large sacs protruded and from these she extracted a viscous* yellow liquid which would become famous throughout the West as castoreum, one of the most gratifying odors in the natural world.

*viscous [VISS-cuss]: thick; not flowing easily

Kneading the castoreum into the mud and mixing in a few grasses to make the cake adhere, she placed it carefully so that its odor would penetrate in all directions, and when she had set out nine of these—for this was a spot worth preserving and protecting—she stopped and tested the results of her labor. She swam upstream and down, and wherever she went she got the clear signal that this stretch of water belonged to a beaver who intended holding it.

She became, that summer, a capable beaver, lively in

her pursuit of things she required. The limestone cavern became not only a place of refuge but also a satisfactory home. She built three secret escape hatches, one leading a good twenty feet inland from the bank of the creek, so that if a bear or wolf did take her by surprise, she could dive into it and make her way back to her home before the predator knew where she had gone.

The cycle of her life, however, was still incomplete. By herself she would not build a dam, nor a lodge either, for they were needed primarily for the rearing of young. She could survive in the limestone cave, but without the act of building a lodge with a mate, she was still an outcast.

This did not prevent her from attending herself as carefully as ever. Each day, when the sun was low, she perched on the bank overlooking her domain and preened. She did this by using the two peculiar toes on each of her hind legs; the nails on these toes were split so as to form small combs, and these she dragged through her pelt until even the slightest irregularity was removed. Then she took oil from her body and carefully applied it to each part of her coat, combing it in deeply until her fur glistened in shimmering loveliness. No one saw or applauded this grooming, but it was impossible for her to go to bed until she had completed it.

And then, in early autumn when she had given up hope of finding a mate, a shabby beaver seven years old who had lost his family in some catastrophe wandered down the river and turned by chance into her creek. He was by no means a handsome creature; indeed, he was not even acceptable, for a long gash ran down the left side of his face and he had lost the two toes on his left hind leg that he needed for cleaning himself, so that his appearance was disreputable.

As he sashayed* up the creek he detected the markers and realized immediately that a mistake had been made. The creek spot looked inviting but any flood from the river would wash it away. He looked about for the family which occupied it to warn them of the danger they faced, and after a while he saw the head of the owner breaking through the surface. She swam out to him cautiously and looked for his mate, while he looked for hers. There was a period of motionless silence. He was tired and winter was at hand.

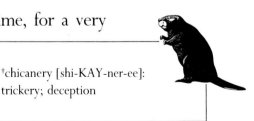

*sashayed [sash-SHADE]: strutted; pranced

They stared at each other for a long time, for a very long time, and each knew all there was to know. There would be no illusions, no chicanery.†

†chicanery [shi-KAY-ner-ee]: trickery; deception

It was he who broke the silence. By the way he looked and moved his tail he indicated that this spot was no place to build a dam.

With a fierce toss of her head she let him know that this was where she would live. And she led him underwater to the entrance of her secret cave and showed him the escape hatches and how she planned to link it to the lodge and the dam, but still he was not satisfied, and when they surfaced, he started to swim to a much safer spot, and she followed, chattering and slamming her tail and halting in disgust as he left her premises.

In the morning he swam back and indicated hesitantly that she was welcome to accompany him if she would consent to build their dam at a proper site.

Again she abused him, protesting furiously and snapping at him, driving him from her water, and that afternoon he came back quietly with a length of aspen in his teeth. Diving to the bottom of the creek, he fastened it to the floor with mud, the first construction in their new home.

It was then September and they set to work with a passion. They labored all night, dragging trees and branches into the stream, weighting them with mud, and gradually

building the whole construction high enough to check the flow of water. Again and again as they worked he betrayed his doubt that the dam they were building would hold, but she worked with such fervor that he swallowed his precautions.

When the two beavers were satisfied that the dam would impound the water necessary for their establishment, she began tying branches and tree lengths into the bottom, weighting them with rocks and mud and other trees, and it was now that she realized that in the building of the dam she had done most of the work. He was great on starting things, and showed considerable enthusiasm during the first days, but when it came time for doing the hard, backbreaking work, he was usually absent.

She had to acknowledge that she had accepted a lazy mate, one who could not be cured, but instead of infuriating her, this merely spurred her to greater effort. She worked as few beavers, an industrious lot, had ever worked, lugging huge trunks of trees and slapping mud until her paws ached. She did both the planning and the execution, and when the pile from which their lodge would be constructed was nearly finished, and she was eleven pounds lighter than when she started, he indicated for the final time that when the floods came, this would all vanish. She made no response, for she knew that just as she had done most of the building this time, she would have to do it again if floods ever did come.

When the pile in the middle of the small lake behind the dam was completed, they dived to the bottom and began the gratifying task of cutting entrances into it, and providing sleeping levels above the waterline, and places for kits when they came, and digging connecting runways to the secret chamber, and at this planning he was a master, for he had built lodges before.

Only a few days remained before the freeze, and this period they spent in a burst of superenergy, stripping bark and storing it for their winter's food. Where eating was concerned, he was willing to work, and in the end they had a better lodge than any other on the creek, and better provisioned too.

In the early days of winter, when they were frozen in, they mated, and in spring, after she gave birth to four lovely babies, the river produced a flood which washed away the dam and most of the lodge. He grunted as it was happening, but she rescued the babies and took them to higher ground, where a fox ate one.

As soon as the floods receded, she began to rebuild the dam, and when it was finished, she taught the babies how to help rebuild the lodge, which took less effort.

They then enjoyed four good years in their tight little kingdom, but on the fifth, sixth, and seventh years there were floods, the last of such magnitude that the whole establishment was erased. This was enough for him, and he spent considerable time upstream looking for a better site, but when he found one, she refused to move. He found her marking the corners of her estate with castoreum and teaching her children how to start erecting a higher and better dam.

He halted at the edge of her territory and watched as this stubborn little creature proceeded with her engineering, making the same mistakes, dooming her dam to the same destruction.

He was now fifteen years old, an advanced age for a beaver, and she treated him with respect, not requiring him to haul logs or do much actual construction on the lodge. He snapped at the kits when they placed branches carelessly, indicating that if he were in charge he would not accept such sloppy workmanship. As he aged, his face grew uglier, with the scar predominating, and he moved with crotchets and limps, and one day while he was helping girdle some cotton-woods, he failed to detect a wolf approaching and would have been snatched had he not been bumped toward the safety tunnel by his mate.

That year there was no flood.

Then one day in early autumn when the food was safely in and the lodge never more secure, she happened to wander up the tunnel into the secret place which the family had so much enjoyed, and she found him lying there on the limestone ledge, his life gone. She nudged him gently, thinking that he might be asleep, then nuzzled him with affection to waken him for their evening swim through the lake they had built and rebuilt so many times, but he did not respond, and she stayed with him for a long time, not fully comprehending what death signified, unwilling to accept that it meant the end of their long and necessary companionship.

In the end the children took the body away, for it was

no longer of any use, and automatically she went about the job of gathering food. Dimly she sensed that now there could be no more babies, no more kits playing in the limestone chamber and scampering down the runways.

She left the security of the lodge and went to each of the compass points and to the salient* ridges in between, and at each she scooped up a handful of mud and mixed it with grass and kneaded in a copious† supply of castoreum, and when the job was done she swam back to the middle of her lake and smelled the night air.

*salient [SAY-lee-ent]: jutting out; projecting; protruding; prominent

†copious [COE-pee-us]: ample; abundant; in a large amount

This was her home, and nothing would drive her from it, neither loneliness nor the attack of otters nor the preying of wolves nor the flooding of the river. For the home of any living thing is important, both for itself and for the larger society of which it is a part.

FIVE

Throughout these stories we have seen certain similarities between families of the wild and human ones, between the developmental stages of animal children and those of human children. These likenesses draw us closer to the lives and struggles of the wild creatures who share this planet with us, and they give us an opportunity to better understand ourselves in the process.

But there are many aspects of animal families

that seemingly have no human counterparts whatever, and one of these is the great massing together that occurs in the lives of migratory birds, fish, mammals, and insects. Species as varied as the African wildebeest, the sockeye salmon, and the monarch butterfly each herd themselves and embark upon a perilous and protracted journey, pressing on as with a single mind. Our understanding of these migrations is still quite imperfect, but we do see their purpose: The species must survive.

In these animal migrations we can see an entire civilization in miniature. Even though the mass is in constant motion, some characteristics remain fixed. The unchangeable command of nature, which governs families of penguins and wolves and eagles and beavers, lies also at the heart of every migration: The species must endure. If the unique characteristics of caribou would be more surely perpetuated through small families or independence and isolation, then that is how caribou would live. But what we see as an unmerciful and senseless trek across the wilderness is, for the caribou, its guarantee of continued existence, for while some offspring will be killed, others will survive. And that is what nature commands of all species in all forms of community. The young must be born; they must be nourished and protected; if they die, the species is doomed. Nature invests everything in its children, and then it provides small families and great migrations to protect its investment.

In the following excerpt from The Endless Migrations, Roger Caras—television correspondent, syndicated columnist, and author of more than fifty books about animals and their environments—follows a massive herd of caribou as they make their annual migration to new feeding grounds hundreds of miles across the treeless Arctic expanse *known as the tundra. Among his other works about animals—both wild and domesticated—and about the many ways that humans are destroying animals' natural habitats are* Animals in Their Places, A Celebration of Cats/Dogs, Death As a Way of Life, Source of Thunder, Sockeye, *and* The Forest.

CARIBOU HERD

from *The Endless Migrations*

ROGER CARAS

The caribou is an animal of elastic strengths. It is resilient and adapts well to wolf and man, even though man has added to his arsenal* at an exponential rate. The wolves, however, stood still; their technology of death did not improve. Their tactics were ancient, their needs unchanging, they had no commerce, no new reasons for taking

> *arsenal [AR-sen-al]: supply or store of weapons; here, the many tools humans use to hunt and kill

more animals in new ways. The wolf killed, strenuously, to live while man superimposed the supposed legitimacy of sport and after that the vague* claim of integrity and salvation. Still the caribou traveled past the firing lines, thundered past settlements, even used roads and railbeds where they existed on the soggy tundra. Their numbers continued to fall, but without the power of oversight and with no understanding or concern for their own population dynamics, the caribou pushed on. They were locked into ways as unyielding as that of the salmon, the monarch butterfly, and the gray whale. Although opportunistic and adaptable when cleared roads offered a path in the right direction, still the caribou adopted their direction first and held to that rigidly no matter what they encountered.

*vague [VAYG]: not clear or specific

Even in the farthest reaches of the north there is a time of joy. Summer heat and the curtains of hungry insects are gone for the year and the harshness is still weeks away. The days are warm enough for every animal to move with ease and pleasure, yet cool evenings signal the time ahead and frost glitters across the landscape to greet each morning's sun like enormous ice sheets shattered and strewn. At traditional places, usually in sheltered valleys where trails have been trodden for thousands of years, cranberries and blueberries and other autumn crops ripen. Late salmon runs fill the streams. Ptarmigan† move toward higher ground in anticipation of the coming snow and

†ptarmigan [TAR-mih-gan]: a type of grouse that has feathered feet and inhabits cold northern regions

the sky fills with waterfowl seeking their winter ranges far to the south. Swans cluster in surprising thousands, with mallard, goldeneye, and mergansers all among them. Wigeon, old squaw,* ducks of sweet water and of the sea, moving southward and facing thousands of miles of flight before coming to rest for yet another winter, are all part of one vast current in the sky. The Arctic is like a huge engine of life, and each fall it pulses and pours forth living product and lends it to distant and warmer lands, though under contract for a single season only.

*mallard, goldeneye, mergansers [mur-GAN-sirs], wigeon [WIJ-un], old squaw: types of ducks

All manner of birds facing monumental flights were now layered with fat, and so indeed were the caribou that began to move, thickly furred and armed against the harshness from which they could not flee on wings. They would face the ice storms, become half buried in snow-driven winds, yet stand fast to live and reproduce again the following spring. The birds had fat for flight, which they would burn at the rapid pace of avian metabolism,† while the slower mammals would build the corresponding fat to help them hold in place, slowly absorbing what they needed while using the outstanding balance for insulation.

†avian metabolism [AA-vee-an met-TAB-uh-liz-um]: the way birds convert food and fat to energy

As autumn colors blazed across the tundra, the largest of the caribou found it difficult to regulate body temperatures through the layers of back fat that held in the heat. They breathed rapidly, flicked their ears against the last, lingering black flies, and ate some more. More fat was needed; every ounce was an investment against the poor death of a harsh winter and an unprepared animal. The winter that was coming was a force without limit. Nothing could stop it. The caribou could only prepare and wait and eat beyond the demands of immediate need. The drive to engorge was the hunger of life, the need to live and to move the pattern of caribou life forward for yet another generation.

There is a herd mindlessness to animals in mass movement. A single caribou or a dozen might turn to stare at a pair of wolves and worry about their stalking movements. A few caribou might flee at the mere sight of hunters. But when the hoofed creatures form into vast floods, when they coalesce* into massed thousands, the mind of the single animal is overwhelmed, absorbed by the sheer magnitude of the many. A herd of thousands of animals will ignore the wolves. The mass presses on, profoundly content that it can spare its losses. A single animal cannot spare some part of itself, a single cow cannot spare her calf, but a large herd can. It is the quandary† of the mass mind, the herdiness that dulls the senses of the individual. Perhaps, and we speculate here, there are leaders at the front of the movement who worry about the wolves on the horizon ahead, but behind them come the thousands that are made so secure by their fellow creatures pressing in through touch and scent and

*coalesce [coe-ah-LESS]: come together as one body; unite

†quandary: puzzlement; here, the unknowable forces that are at work

72

sound that they are mindless, pounding toward winter and the drive to survive it.

The thundering caribou may veer slightly or even occasionally turn if their leaders turn, but generally, in their mindless push toward the coming season, the herd ignores wolves, hunters, all else, and listens only to some primal force. That force, the coming of migration, controls the mass mind of the herd. And when the antlered herds and the flights of birds and the plankton* swarms do not appear, the predators in turn die in the agony of hunger, cannibalism, and disease.

*plankton: floating or drifting plant and animal organisms

The caribou followed an ancient pattern. At the end of July the big summer herds had splintered, moved apart. The animals had gone off singly or in small herds, bachelors, cows, and the young alone at last, each to find others of their kind and to feed leisurely together in the time of Arctic plenty. But as the air began to chill, first at night and, with each successive day, later into morning, the animals began coming together again. Two bulls, solitary for much of the summer, began feeding near each other, then were joined by two more. Their antlers were now full grown, and it remained only to strip away the velvet that concealed their new hardness and their pointed tips. Bulls gathered near every tree, every bush, in the all but treeless land and rubbed against the branches. Bubbles of blood showed through the velvet, but the soft cover fell away in tatters, and the vegetable sap and berry juice and the blood from the tiny vessels of the now fallen velvet slowly darkened the antlers as they were tempered for battle. Farther south other deer were following the same pattern, and nearby in overlapping range the giant of all deer, the moose, were also embarked on the same task.

Where two caribou had grazed there were ten, then a hundred. After wandering in circles for several days they began to move with purpose. Those on high ground flowed down toward the riverbanks, where the vegetation would last longer and survive the night frosts. In the willow thickets they encountered the moose and moved away, leaving the solitary giants the peace and space they demanded. Rivers appeared and were crossed, some torrents running hard enough to claim lives. Cows and immature animals were now flowing in the same general direction as the bulls, but the

bulls still kept apart. The bands, not yet a large massed herd, were often in sight of one another, and both began to encounter wolves, creatures that had learned down the millennia* where the caravan would invariably crest a certain riverbank, where they would compress their growing masses through ancient cuts in the land.

*millennia [mih-LEN-ee-uh]: many thousands of years

And now the bulls began shoving one another, engaged in what appeared to be good-natured games. Their future lay in combat for the possession of the cows. So the bulls moved and mock-fought and moved some more. Immature animals and cows maintained their parallel tracks.

Each night the frost froze harder, each morning it was slower to disperse. Then one night a blizzard struck. The animals and the land were snow-covered by the time the late-rising sun appeared. The colors of the tundra, explosive only a few days or a week before, were faded and gone. Now the landscape was white. As the caribou thundered on, their numbers growing by the hour, flights of birds crossed high overhead, pushing south before the next blizzard struck. The calls of the geese and swans and lesser birds echoed against the ground and whistled through the wind like one musical theme that is working its way through another. It was a fabric of sound that came and went, whistled and hummed, until the symphony of descending winter encompassed all.

The immense pattern of lakes and ponds that dotted the tundra was now frozen, but there were few with ice thick enough to sustain the pounding of a caribou herd. The animals crashed through the splintering ice, and frozen water squirted up around them like diamond dust and silver rain. A few animals foundered* but most pushed on. It was only a matter of a few more days before temperatures became consistently low enough to turn the water into a pavement as hard as anything that man could create. The lakes and ponds and rivers would turn from umber and earth to silver, blue, and white, and the herds would use them as avenues of convenience.

*foundered: became lame or fell

Hunters formed their ranks along the migratory path, fired into the herds, and moved about later collecting their kill. Those wounded animals that managed to pull ahead of the hunters and stay with the herd would begin to fall back in a day or two. Wolves would soon pull them down, but those that fell before the wolf packs struck would be found by bears, grizzlies of the barren ground that rolled on the carcasses to absorb their smell, then snuggled their great snouts into the entrails to pull them apart at leisure. No part of a caribou would be wasted. Magpies, crows, ravens, and foxes would move in on the fallen animals as well and pull away flesh that had come to them so effortlessly.

By the middle of October a restlessness began to move through the congregation of bulls. They grunted rhythmically, their necks now swollen, their sharpened antlers set for battle. Younger bulls learned quickly that they were outclassed, and only the larger, fuller, and more brutally aroused animals

remained in position to battle for the cows. Skidding and slipping, tearing up turf and snow with antlers and hooves, the bulls fought across the increasingly broken ground. The triumphant bulls moved off to join the now receptive cows. In the meantime the caribou continued to move, their paths intercepting, their numbers growing, and their purpose ever more clear as they moved to where the snow cover might be thin, the lichens* and

*lichens [LYE-kenz]: small plants in leaflike, crustlike, or branching forms that grow on rocks and trees

grasses beneath more readily grazed. It was now a time to survive. Mating occurred, young were promised for another year, but now the winter must be endured—and this, then, was the real reason for the migration. As the mating eased off, the bulls wandered away, joined each other, sought deep, quiet cuts where there was any vegetation at all. It was cold every hour now; every minute of the day and night it would become colder still. The herd was about to face the ultimate test. The best would emerge in the spring and disperse back toward the areas from which the thundering mass had come. A circle was half drawn.

The migration of caribou covered hundreds of miles, making it quite probably the longest overland migration by a terrestrial animal now known. They moved from an area where willow branches had been stripped to one where grasses and lichens could still be anticipated under a covering of snow. They followed that primordial* route because their instincts, honed over thousands of generations, had pushed them to it. But to know to move, to know to seek food, to know the time is right is not necessarily to know the way. There lies a mystery not yet solved.

*primordial [pry-MOR-dee-al]: from the very beginning of time

There is good reason to believe that magnetism is a factor, perhaps the most profound factor, but we do not know for certain that such is the case. The earth's position had changed, and the animals had changed in relation to the sun, so there could be visual clues. There are prevailing winds, possibly half-remembered land shapes and forms, altitudes in sequence, and, in the higher latitudes, cosmic radiation far more intense than in areas near the equator. Incoming radiation strikes the earth's magnetic shield and slides around the planet like quicksilver beads on a giant slope, coming to earth near the poles. Intensity of radiation may offer clues, but we cannot say for certain how the caribou find their way. They do find it, though, surely, unerringly, in predictable wave upon wave, to complete that first half of the circle. It is the first half because it is during that movement that mating, the future, is assured.

INDEX